balm

Compiled by

Raven's Quoth Press

PENSIVE REFLECTIONS

Balm First Edition
Balm Second Edition

Dream First Edition
Dream Second Edition

Psythur First Edition

EDGAR ALLAN POE-INSPIRED COLLECTION

Evermore First Edition
Evermore Second Edition

ROMANCE COLLECTION

Cherish First Edition
Tempest First Edition

INDIVIDUAL COLLECTIONS

Songs of the Underland & Other Macabre Machinations
by Kurt Newton

Follow us at:
linktr.ee/TheRavensQuothPress

THE RAVENS QUOTH PRESS 243

"Remember your survival, your journey, your scars deserve to be treasured too."

— "Kintsugi" by Nikita Gill

CAROL EDWARDS is a northern California native transplanted to southern Arizona. She lives and works in relative seclusion with her books, plants, and pets (+ husband). She enjoys a coffee addiction and raising her succulent army. Her work has recently appeared in *Open Skies Quarterly* and Red Penguin Books.

Instagram: @practicallypoetical

Tattoo

by Carol Edwards

Prints trip down my inner arm

drip down
Through my fingertips

Driplets, drops
red memories

Tiny dots of light
trail after me

Constellations

In a crushing vacuum

squeeze air out my lungs
oceans leak past
lacrimal dams, avalanches
crash at concave glass
spill out spillways, flooding planes

other hand clutches

at the long line gash

running upstream, rushing

raw and rasping along my veins

Light stabs in prism shards

Rainbows tainted gray

Out damn spot splotch stain

Crimson clover puddled gore

pooled on the tile floor

My insides melted down, smelted

sunshine hopes dissolved

into bone dust pressed on my scarred face

unseeing eyes trace ghosts haunting us

Old Sweatshirt

by Carol Edwards

You pretend its arms are my arms
Wrapped around your waist

My chest to your back
Keeping you warm on cold days

The red thread from my heart knit
Into something you hide yourself in

Tuck your knees up underneath
And your hands in the sleeves

Until nothing but your toes peek
Out, maybe your nose

Nestled in the collar, smells of my cologne
The tag brushing your neck is my breath

A ghost all that's left
From what short time I called you mine

Lips to your hair pressed
The memory as fleeting as a breeze

To desert heat brings relief
Or rain to parched ground where seeds sleep

Comatose til by its kiss awaked
Sleeping princess cursed

To push through stone and ash
Rebuild the ruins fire left in her path

When the Monster Under Your Bed Has Become Your Friend

by Carol Edwards

Inspired by Linda D Addison's "How to Recognize a Demon Has Become Your Friend."

Another day done
another wasted chance;
another wound, future scar,
pinprick
or gash
skin bruise, heart bruise—it all blurs as one.

Crawl battered into bed,
the monster underneath
reaches for my hand.
He doesn't understand
why I tell him, "Wait. Wait. There's still
some good somewhere.
I can't give up yet."

Perhaps one day,
as monsters do,
he'll watch you stir another ruse
and disregard the words I said.
Instead,
in darkness as you sleep,

he'll creep his coils around your feet,
python slow, until
he's swallowed you in his grip;
jointed spindle legs
your chest will rip,

his aim to hold in taloned hand

your heart, still beating.

Into it he'll sink his fangs, a ripened plum,

your blood the nectar he desires,

eyes aglow with molten fires.

Your throat he'd crush

with a single blow;

silent your screams as he

devours your eyes, such delicacies.

Patiently so far he bides,

sensing the slow sap of hope I hold.

Once it's gone,

and under the bed I crawl,

safer there than prison walls,

through my hair his claws will run

until I sleep;

and then your time has come.

Our Hungers

by Carol Edwards

all within us hide, sedated lightning
quietly caged,
icy burn rumbles and scrapes
a tamed dream rage, soon lulled
back to sleep, leaking tempests
through our eyes,
until one too many breaks—
trusts, hopes, hearts, bones—
cracks the muting haze

then like dragons wake, screams
un-numbed, and we gut
ourselves from inside trying
to contain the beasts
who starve like we for warmth, rest,
peace
dying a little each day
the will to fight slowly chipped away.

I'm the Lungs Now

by Carol Edwards

"Tell you what,"

I say to myself,

"you finish this email

and as reward you can go make

your baked potato—

it'll be done about 5

and you'll be hungry by then."

But I'm hungry now.

Not just in my belly, that'll keep

for an hour;

hungry under my skin,

in the dark somewhere

I never let people in, not really.

Hungry for LIFE,

hungry for the love and the soul

of someone who will feed me willingly

after seeing the dark,

their love for me a power I use to keep

them here,

my love for them

what tethers, brings them back again,

like I used to do for ones

hungry for me

but not for *me*—just what I'd give

to keep their attention, so easily withdrawn,

so easily thrown away,

when that was all I had to keep breathing.

Now I'm hungry

but not like them;

give me your love and soul to eat—

the real stuff,

none of this cotton candy fluff—

and to you I'll give air

so you can breathe,

finally

Last. Words

by Carol Edwards

I wasn't thinking about you when I died.

I was thinking about me,

about the unbearable cruelty

of having to stay trapped here

in the cage I shaped for myself,

not knowing what my hands made

until too late, put myself in

never to escape.

I wasn't thinking about you, how the news

might sucker punch you in your gut,

how you might feel cold, empty,

guilty you hadn't seen the signs,

then burning rage at how dare I

declare I love you then leave you behind,

the pieces of yourself you gave

with me in a grave.

I wasn't thinking about you waiting for me

so many years,

to realize what to me felt air-tight

you could break from outside,

and you doubting why I never asked—

Until now, I hadn't known I could.

Extracted

by Carol Edwards

You broke my heart into more manageable pieces,

ground them up fine, one by one;

steeped them in boiled pain, a decade long test,

then complained when the juice tasted of bitterness.

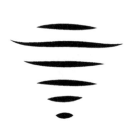

BRIANNA MALOTKE is a member of the Horror Writers Association. You can find her most recent work in the anthologies *Beautiful Tragedies 2*, *The Dire Circle*, and *Under Her Skin*, a Women in Horror Poetry Showcase. Looking ahead, she has poetry within both *Tempest* and *Cherish*, by Ravens Quoth Press.

Website: brimalotke.wixsite.com/malotkewrites

Graveyard Whispers

by Brianna Malotke

Withered roses and scratched headstones
Were her immediate thoughts
As she stood alone at the edge of the entrance
Of the cemetery.

With the weight of her offering
Heavy on her shoulders,
She took off towards the grave,
No longer empty.

Making her way through the crowded
Plots, passing grave markers
And stone statues, she finally
Found the name she needed.

Standing in silence,
Every memory of their
Shared moments
Flashed through her mind.

For a brief, fleeting moment,
She thought the faint scent
Of her lover's perfume was
In the crisp autumn air.

A piece of her soul,
The love of her life,
Lay buried six feet beneath
Where her feet stood.

Aching and hallow, yet
Her heart remained strong
As she told their story to the
Surrounding graves.

Her whispers carried off by the wind.

In Good Company

by Brianna Malotke

I wish you could keep me company

as I brave the emptiness of the afterlife.

My soul lingering here as you stand

at the headstone, recently placed,

and stare at the carved stone, displaying

a name you can't believe. With each tear

I see your heartache, and silently scream

your name, but all you hear is the wind.

And so I choose to stay here, patiently waiting,

In case you come back to visit my grave.

Indefinite Love

by Brianna Malotke

Every night spent with you, wrapped

In love, was such a blessing, for no one

Could ever compare to you—a true dream.

Every day passed spent with you by my side.

Such warmth and romance in every little

Movement and touch—a true dream.

It's been mere months since you've left.

Every moment passes in agony, your perfume

Lingers in the house, unsure about my future

But I know I'll never bury another true love.

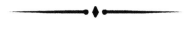

JOHN DRUDGE is a social worker working in the field of disability management and holds degrees in social work, rehabilitation services, and psychology. He is the author of four books of poetry: *March* (2019), *The Seasons of Us* (2019), *New Days* (2020), and *Fragments* (2021). His work has appeared widely in numerous literary journals, magazines, and anthologies internationally. John is also a Pushcart Prize and Best of the Net nominee and lives in Caledon Ontario, Canada with his wife and two children.

Hard Streets

by John Drudge

Picked clean
As a skeleton
Drifting with the tide
On a meridian
Of wisdom
And faith
Through the illusion
Of time
Washing over
The blood of dreams
And falling into
A volatile permutation
Of shrinking space
As I strike out
Toward the receding sun
Pale as cold water
Flooding
The hard streets

Rag and Bones

by John Drudge

I sit upon the pylons again
Where the streets of the world
Meet those of the mind
And I am at that place
Where poets go
Where pilgrims hide in the confines
And soldiers explore
The warrens of the soul
I am at that place
In my own eternity
Where words and time
Bleed into something new
And dip deep into the river
That winds us through
And through

Offshore

by John Drudge

It's a worthwhile experience
To sit back and listen
As we become
Obsessed with birth
And the repetition
Of time
Lasting immortality
And fresh visions
Of life
Drowning
In new beginnings
While drifting
From cape to cape
Along the rocky coast
Of forgiveness
In a riptide
Of lost chances
On the cold
Whispering sea

Drifting

by John Drudge

Across the reeds
Through the marsh
By the bending willow
In the clearing
With the day breaking
Wishes on rocks
In the creek
In the distance
Where intuition
Introspection
And the ogling of regret
Turn up the volume
On our most
Wandering thoughts

In the Aftermath

by John Drudge

The inclinations
Of decline
In colorific style
Where the little things
Of living
Are largely meaningless
Where vengeance
And hatred
Are tasted on the tongue
And beggars
Left to the cold
Twist and push
To get a better look
At the genius
Of demise
Disrobing new
And tormented saviors
Of our salvation
And imagining
The unimaginable
As the rules of heaven Break

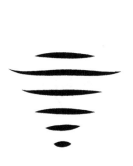

STEVEN FORTUNE is a resident of Canada and a graduate of Acadia University (English Literature/History). He has released five poetry collections to date, edited several works by others for his publisher, and has also appeared on CBC Radio, while his work has been featured and read on several radio programs.

The Incredibly Shrunken Man

by Steven Fortune

How'd you like a laugh?
Oh no
Not from me
Not with all the guidelines
preconceived then refined
like a sporting rulebook
Any cue to laugh is doomed
to a failed smuggle
over my absorption border
Immunity to manifestation
was fortified by young death
raked over decades of
punch line padding
until the line between the addict
and the volunteer became
a moving target
Foil humor came to be
too easily unwrapped by
the vampiric appetites

of class structure overlords
Sorry
Too dramatic?
Trying too hard I reckon
to extract a profit
from the definition of traumatic
I exhausted too much
material
in the ghostwriting done
for sordid hordes of enterprising
comedians
To think now
of all the chest-beating braggarts
I sold myself short to
And to think I cashed in
reflexive tutelage
for receipts of credibility
No
Pluck the sugar-scented fertilizer fruits
of another garden
There is only drama for you here
And your pockets will betray you
for entertaining curiosity
with your heart's grimy double-down
in tow

Long Division

by Steven Fortune

All of my equations
are handicapped
Hospice infusers now
Every moment
reset
only by conscience
strait-jacketed
in gratuitous silence
No more reliance on
intransitive scarcity
Only the act of seeking
survived with feeling
That's how I've learned
to approximate
how it would feel
to attend my funeral
not in phantom
regalia
but live
Living and hiding again

AVERY HUNTER invented writing, the quokka (but not its propensity for sacrificing its young to predators), and mudguards for bicycles (after an unfortunate incident one muddy Monday morning). Now they teach tarantulas how to make a perfect mimosa.

linktr.ee/AuthorAveryHunter

Storm Eunice

by Avery Hunter

Eunice, she screams
Winds thrashing at the beaches.
Toppling trees
and scattering peaches.

Stranding yachts
while buildings fall
And there she is
in the middle of the squall

She feels the deluge
My beauty, my queen
Tears travel her face
So angry, yet so serene

She purges the black
From her soul
When the rain stops
She's regained control

ARIK MITRA lives in Kolkata, India. An IT professional by day, he has been writing for a little more than two years. He writes mainly poetry and short stories in English and Bengali (his mother tongue). His works have been published by Clarendon House Publications, Red Penguin Books and literary journals like *Lothlorien Journal, The Quiver Review, Writers and Readers Magazine* and more.

Facebook:@arik.mitra.927

Vindication Has Glimpsed

by Arik Mitra

Raked,
this squire of holy Deceit,
Irons rub against slate
with cacophony.
Comes too natural to that tongue—lies.

Like ash, diffuse with the urn that hosts
Death, death, all my eyes see
Ghastly chamber below your unkempt hair,
no tissue below
that black, velvet garb,
just a hollow. Abysmal it is.
O! I cannot speak! I cannot sing!
Vindication has glimpsed!
on a heavy head in midst of ears hot,
Nero stands with hysteric eyes,
wide they are,
stands on the porch he,
and plays the lyre, while embers dance
in quaking streets of a burning Rome.

Vindication Glimpsed Again

by Arik Mitra

Blindfolded demons,

in flexible cages—darkness they abide,

yet burn.

Appalling ashen petals,

that slithery cold fabric

of their skin.

As the bars they touch,

black fire scars.

Upon those screams

of pain—rage.

Immersed in Vindication's lust

Yes, Vindication has glimpsed again

Again! Inner Archfiend wakes

to ravish, plunder,

destroy all remnants

of humane relic, as Sanity descends

An inscrutable descent,

seeking revenge. That blind rawness

of blood curdling vows

stands to kill. Hatred's slay

count never stops at one.

Man's blood, addictive wine

in decanters, Hell's glasswork.

Drums silenced, silence is loud enough.

Light's permeated years

Such are the woes

of Vindication's victory cry

Seekers lose sense of all else—

his ears, his body, no years remain to him

Yet he hears that cry.

Cries he, in tears, hearing nothing—

nothing, but that cry.

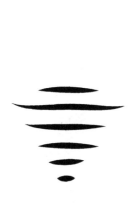

BERNARDO VILLELA has had poetry published by Entropy, Zoetic Press, and Bluepepper and others. He's had fiction published with *Coffin Bell Journal, The Dark Corner, Page & Spine* and others. You can read more about these and various other pursuits at www.miller-villela.com.

Gauze-World

by Bernardo Villela

In a diaphanous
Bergmanesque
black & white
existence, he
steps into the
room. Lying
at my side
his face turns
into mine and
mine into his.

Into the gauze-world
we dove, set to drown,
cloud-sheet billowing,
brewing storms and
tenuous calms that
would never last long.
Greyed blue-eyes stung
my soul & split my heart.
Ears burnt by his incisive
words & most acerbic barbs.

Speaking each other's words
misunderstanding all we say.
Our roles could be inverted
or we could be in other bodies

and our conversations would always
end the same. The confusion,
deviated our psychic septums,
frayed our corpora callosa. So
we did not speak, but we ran
lines and practiced our
amorous embouchure.

Through utter silence spiders crawl,
blind corpse-memories walk and
threaten our solitude with their most
hateful solicitude.

The world's silence

sprung from God muteness punctures

our eardrums. Tongues tied now in

knots that will not be loosed, he & I

clutch onto one another sheltering

each other from the rising tides of

sorrow, that engulf our shores, placid

no more, our island's erasure pending,

an oceanic interment nigh.

Souls bruised,

battered. Psyches hurt. The accumulated

weight of lives ill-lived weigh us down,

decreasing our buoyancy. Wretched wights

are we who even alone cannot be free.

If

only the island in its charcoal and

argentine tones had always been

here & we had always lived here

together, then this tempest in a

cracked teapot might not be

what brought us death

both as a unit and as

individuals. Brine

swallowed

whole the

two of

us.

CATHERINE A. MACKENZIE Cathy's writings can be found in numerous print and online publications. She writes all genres but invariably veers toward the dark—so much so her late mother once asked, "Can't you write anything happy?" (She can!)

Cathy divides her time between West Porters Lake and Halifax, Nova Scotia, Canada.

Website: writingwicket.wordpress.com

Following the Path

by Catherine A. Mackenzie

He grasps my cold limp hand
And I follow into the forest deep.
The cerulean ceiling lunges
And tall trees form our walls,
Our barrier from the world.

I'm swept within a hollow garden
Where moss swells around us,
Sticky and sweet and sickly.
Is it a miracle or a mirage?
Perhaps it's both; perhaps it's neither.

His warmth delves into my depths,
Tingling nerves and caressing bones,
A rush like a speeding freight train,
Determined, yet silent in the night,
Knowing its end, aware of surroundings.

Lost in acres of wilderness,
I scan the blazing landscape from afar,
Amid the hush of nature's songs.
The world is mute and nothing but
The chorus of your breath chimes with mine.

Again in the distance is that train
Lumbering down the tracks to somewhere,
Its roaring refrain haunting the night.
Dragon breath swirls and sways
Before disappearing into the stars.

Then life is silent once more. I'm at peace
In the dark where only angels tread,
Dreams and nightmares quashed forever.
There's nothing, yet there's everything—
Everything but your breath mingling with mine.

CHRISTINE M. DU BOIS is an anthropologist with poems in a dozen anthologies and online magazines, including *Central Texas Writers and Beyond 2021* and the *Valiant Scribe Literary Journal*. Poems are forthcoming in *Psychological Perspectives*, in the Canary Literary Magazine, and in the Red Penguin Press's *Words for the Earth*.https://linktr.ee/AuthorAveryHunter

What She Knows

by Christine M. Du Bois

Her paperbark legs know.
They know menace.
Gestapo rounded up her relatives,
caged them, suffocated them.
On his mottled arms,
her devoted friend wears tattoos
from evil men.
Her stick legs know all this.
Her child-brain screams: run!
Escape the hard rails of this
hospital bed.
But she can't move her brittle legs,
blue-black from insufficient blood flow—
so this must be a prison.
An undeserved prison—
so it must be a camp.
It makes *sense* to spit the applesauce
into her caretaker's face.
She can taste something else in it.
Medicine, her son and his wife tell her.
You should finish the applesauce, they say.
But this is a death prison, and they are the guards,

and the "helpers" they send are henchmen,
so surely the applesauce
is actually a poison.
She knows. Her stiff twig legs know.
They know about hatred.
Everything else now, they've forgotten.
She moans and whimpers.
Why have they done this to her?
Not her legs; they are useless but innocent.
The others.
What did they do to her legs
to trap her this way?
You can't tell her there isn't evil involved.
She knows.

Mute

by Christine M. Du Bois

She is pummelled
by loss upon loss upon loss,
beaten bloodless.
You cannot hear her wild cry
because, neck bent,
eyes downcast,
she cannot bear her own crying,
and so is soundless.
How can such beauty
contain such pain?
How can such sadness
carry the weight
of incandescent grace?
She glides, she waits,
she collapses in upon herself,
folding wings tight
to her perfect feathered ribs.
Sorrow has transmuted
this woman
into a silent swan.

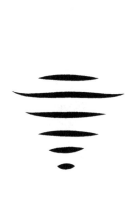

JOSH POOLE is a visual artist and writer working out of a sleepy Virginia town.

Instagram: @shlunka

A Youthful Face in Busy Places

by Josh Poole

Memory's mosaic of missing pieces
Cast cockeyed across the floor
Cannot recall recount what sleep is
To escape in dream's nimble noir

Picture-perfect in yellowed age
A youthful face in busy places
Not yet bereft of beauty's rage
Nor tripped by untied laces

Freckles placed by dogfight aces
In public spaces long and tall and poised faceless
All I can say is
For all the singless songs of birdless thrones
I am imperially alone
Frayed as finest stitch unsewn
Like summer birds in winter flown
I am trite and banal I know

A bastard born of ties now torn
To vessels sailed and pictures paled
I am nobody, as I recall
Swept my arms in scattered empire
Which fills my floor in memory's mire

Was I wrong from the start?
Stray, awry, now apart?
As I lay splayed among pictures dismayed
I miss love's scripture, its soft-sweet tincture
I am alone in arms my own
Among moments loaned by love once sewn

LISA REYNOLDS is a Canadian writer, living east of Toronto, Ontario. Her works are published internationally in anthologies, literary journals, and magazines. She is a member of The Ontario Poetry Society, the Writing Community of Durham Region, and an associate member of The League of Canadian Poets.

In Mourning

by Lisa Reynolds

for Shannon

Light bends under weight
leaves the faithful faithless
as shadows descend like ravens
to peck on brittle bones

Mercy sought mercy found
through Hail Mary prayers
chanted on beaded chain
dangling from open palm

Lost is not forever gone
consoles believer
while beloved soul waits
to rise beneath the ground

**First published in *Lothlorien Poetry Journal,*
February, 2021**

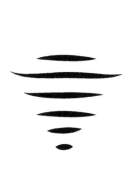

REMA T. DAS, an English teacher and a research scholar resides in India. She has keen interest in writing and has published poems in Literary Garland, Aulos: An Anthology of English Poetry and for the Ekphrastic Review. This poem is on the horror of a child left alone cooing in bed listening to the lullaby sung by her dead mother.

Facebook: @rema.das.5

Horror, Horror!

by Rema T. Das

The half empty glucose drip

Synchronising with the lullaby she sang

Cradling her newborn

Just before she died.

The cooing little child,

Unaware of the lies spun around

The mother's off-white shroud,

Sleeps peacefully beside the mother.

Horror, Horror!

The nurse just cried.

Off to be cremated.

The Father, still unaware

Of the Tragedy

That tiptoed his ostentatious life.

For he too lies at the hospital bed

Struggling for a gulp of air.

The cooing little child

Sleeps peacefully every night

For she still sings the lullaby

Synchronising with the half empty glucose drip.

MICHAEL LEE JOHNSON is a USA and Canadian citizen, now Chicagoland area, is an internationally published poet in 44 countries, several published poetry books, nominated for 4 Pushcart Prize awards and 5 Best of the Net nominations. Over 259 YouTube poetry videos.

I Work My Mind Like Planet Earth

by Michael Lee Johnson

I work my mind

inward into a corner of knots.

Depressed beneath brain bone

I work my words; they overwork me.

Fear is the spirit alone, away from God.

Hospital warriors shake pink pills,

rattle bottles of empty dreams.

I walk my ward down the daily highway;

I work on the roadmap of spirit,

weed out false religions.

Only one God for so many

Twelve-step programs.

I wrap myself around support groups,

look for dependency within their problems.

I publish my poems, life works,

concerns on floor five, psych ward

I edit my redemption,

escape from the laundry room;

run around in circles like planet earth,

looking for my therapist

to seal my comfort.

LYNN WHITE Lynn White lives in north Wales. Her work is influenced by issues of social justice and events, places and people she has known or imagined.

She has been nominated for a Pushcart Prize and a Rhysling Award.

Website: lynnwhitepoetry.blogspot.com

Numbers

by Lynn White

How many times have we had this conversation?

I don't know.

I'm not good with numbers.

And neither are you.

Probably the same number of times

as we've promised not to have it again.

I'm not very good with promises either.

And neither are you

How many times have we made a decision,

a final decision that has convinced us?

Probably never,

As we're still having this conversation.

I'm not very good at decisions either.

And neither are you.

Life has become too complex for us

and the numbers don't add up as we'd like

them to.

We want to stop at two,

But there are other numbers in between.

So, our numbers keep on adding up to nothing.

Nothing except conversations and promises

that we don't want or believe in.

And are unable to end.

First published in *Anti-Heroin Chic*,
August 2016

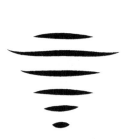

MARK ANDREW HEATHCOTE is an adult learning difficulties support worker. His poetry has been published in many journals, magazines, and anthologies. He resides in the UK and is from Manchester. Mark is the author of *In Perpetuity* and *Back on Earth;* two books of poems published by CTU publishing group, Creative Talents Unleashed.

Obituary of a Dead Poet

by Mark Andrew Heathcote

One day, he'll have a name tag around his big toe
like he belonged someplace, and didn't have far to go.

The slate will be wiped clean, all will be. Reimburse
his Caucasian toe, free of lesions blisters that burst.
All that will be left shall be pages and pages of verse,
and a body that can't afford a burial or the price of a hearse.
And few, other than a priest, will mourn or even attend,
as he can count his friends on one hand, let's not pretend.
The obituaries let the record show
that custom tears did somehow flow,
and angels banked both sides of his coffin, row on row,
and God was in attendance as his guide when he died.
That God removed the name tag.
And God in His heavenly ascendance was by his side.
God was in attendance, and some say, even He cried.

The day they tagged his big toe
like he belonged someplace, and didn't have far to go...

I Guess I'll Just Cherish the Scar

by Mark Andrew Heathcote

Ah, errant star, how distant you are,
how far we have travelled to collide.
Collisions like these are few and far.
So why, love, is it you're unmodified?

Shouldn't my sphere be circling your planet?
Like it was at the start, on fire.
Why now that your heart's core is cold granite?
Why's it jagged rock, my once sweet briar?

Shouldn't my oceans, my moon, be evaporating?
Shouldn't it be liquid mercury expanding?
Why's my heart's flask still emanating
counting the years apart, notwithstanding.

Wish we were closer, my errant star
now we've untangled this relativity.
I guess I'll just cherish the scar,
remember its radioactivity.

Rosa Mundi

by Mark Andrew Heathcote

No excuse given for my short shrift
my heart is too cumbersome to lift.
A mop-headed rose after a shower.
I didn't care for him, didn't flounder.

I've given him his marching orders
he's told his last lie. I can't help but cry
the die has been cast. Bring in the lawyers
I'll show him thorns—a rose not to defy.

I'll cut him to ribbons. And show him
I can be bicolour like Rosa Mundi
the white of my heart and his crimson
splattering's laced imperturbably

Love, Preserving

by Mark Andrew Heathcote

Love's a fruit that requires preserving

if stored; in an equable larder

that isn't hot-tempered, isn't fluctuating

hot then cold—might even keep its ardour.

Spring meandering into another lifetime.

Especially if not bruised or mishandled,

if it's cared for, can see out wintertime—

enchanted, sweetened, heart-gladdened.

But those that are badly handled just-won't-last

and sadly, they will perish as soon as not.

Leaving all your hopes and plans dashed,

and that preserved, beloved fruit will rot.

Somewhere cankers will set in, take hold,

and all you've cherished shall take on mould.

Intervals of Impulse

by Mark Andrew Heathcote

Remember when our hearts beat like cymbals.

Love, must you always be planning ahead,

can't we act on intervals of impulse?

Once we spoke the words of the alphabet

in the silence that transcended language,

and filled a whole encyclopaedia,

every utterance now re-examined.

Nowadays, I feel like anaemia

has drained the blood from my heart and my face.

Where does all our spontaneity go?

Nowadays, I can't get a warm embrace,

and every verbal word is a death blow.

Love, must you always be making up lists?

Does every moment require an eclipse?

Not in Any Haste

by Mark Andrew Heathcote

Oh, how we'd tangle up in those sheets

in them good old days,

darling, do you remember?

And can we rekindle those flames?

I will entice you with my sorrow

but expect to find joyous love

I'll encrypt my darkest passions tomorrow,

if you'd only turn my heart instantly to mush

And then reveal it as a love potion

you've always longed to taste.

You may die in my arms, in devotion

But, my darling, not in any haste.

One Foot Still in the Door

by Mark Andrew Heathcote

His insides are feeling hollowed out
yes, he's been tossed aside before
but this time is different. It's a drought—
his heart is wilting, dried up to the core.

He listens intently for any reason to stay
there are only lies on top of lies.
What was ripe fruit now rots and fades away;
he takes comfort in the mould that slowly dies.

How it lingers to survive, but ultimately expires
this now; how it feels holding her photograph.
The fire is dead. It no longer sparks, or fires,
and her old love letters read like an epitaph.

Love hearts and kisses engraved on a tomb.

He asks himself which way he leans,

but plain as day there's nothing to exhume.

All he needs now; a match and some gasoline.

He asks himself which way he leans,

finding himself with one foot still in the door.

Vying this darkness back into its ravine,

wanting you back more now than before.

Winter Chills

by Mark Andrew Heathcote

Everything in the garden is rosy

until the frost leans against its sharp scythe.

The rose that spent all summer long blowsy;

now it is cold, curled up tightly, heart writhed—

relinquishing the fight with head nodding.

It accepts the love affair's concluded.

A brisk wind, and rain cannonading

against our will, has also intruded.

Like those rattling windowpanes, we close up.

We freeze over, sinking back to our roots.

What can adjudge this poisoned chalice cup

to be charged in you, and me, who dilutes

the warm sunshine in a bare, lifeless tree.

Unadorned, I ask you to still love me.

Cot Death

by Mark Andrew Heathcote

Aloft to my angel, my angel child

that winged, my heart flutters with joy.

I wish to bring ye young one home

and clothe thy bones with flesh and blood

but all I have is gone—my seed is in the grave.

Ye have flowered and died in the spring.

Our little winged soul is ye lost? Lost like sheep

when I count my dying prayers and weep

don't bleat child, don't bleat.

In the holy meadow, sleep, sleep, sleep

until that time again we meet.

It's Easier to Fall in Love

by Mark Andrew Heathcote

Lovers are always forward in what they say,
but when love is old, it gets harder to say,
I love you; please won't you stay?

Dreams hover off the ground when all is new.
But when dreams are old, it's harder to be true.
When your failures aftertaste do come to rue

It's harder to query will there be other chances
it's easier to dream up a fictional courtship dance
it's easier to fall in love and find a new romance
if your heart hasn't dried weeping perchance

One day, you might fall out and be in love again
it easier to fall in love, is all I'm sayin'
if you've no beginning or end, no am or pm
just an open heart and soul—amen.

MARSHA WARREN MITTMAN's memoir, *You Know You Moved to SD from NYC When...* (Scurfpea Publishing), was granted a Western Horizon award. Poetry/essays/short stories, including six *Chicken Soup* tales, were published in America, Britain, Germany, India, and Australia. She's received poetry/prose distinctions in the US and Ireland, and an Alabama residency.

Moorcroft Manor

by Marsha Warren Mittman

That house…that beautiful house

Some say it's haunted you know

Faint images they've seen…of her

The young duchess…just floating

In her cape and gown, down the stairs

In the rose garden, out back by the stream

He died you see, her father

Unexpectedly, without a will

Out boar hunting with guests

When thrown from his horse

Leaving her no dowry, no income

No means whatsoever

And the law, the piteous law
Bequeaths all to the first son
Leaving the girl and her mum
Beggars, so to speak, completely
Dependent for their very lives
Upon the charity of others

The girl's betrothal broken
Of course, without a farthing
What could she possibly expect
And next day she's found floating…
Floating in the stream back of that
Beautiful house her younger brother
Refused to let his mum and sister enter

Candles for Natalie

by Marsha Warren Mittman

It seems to me

The shortest candles

Burn the brightest

That when dark winds

Blow to staunch their

Flames they fight

The hardest to stay lit

So that even if their

Lights are snuffed their

Glow shines on forever

To brighten others' paths

Five Questions

by Marsha Warren Mittman

What is the color of despair
I ask
Of those blind to its pain

What is the sound of hope
I wonder
When pleas for change are ignored

What is the touch of neglect
I shout
To those who turn their backs

What is the taste of anger
I yell
When people cannot feel

What is the smell of death
I cry
At those who walk away

Children's Song

by Marsha Warren Mittman

Come children sing the war-making song

A game of skill and chance and greed

And power across the board game called

    Earth

Come children, war game pawns, sent

By generals dictators war lords to manifest

Capricious bidding and misguided strategy

To blaze, not in glory, but in destruction pain

    Death

To scorch the board game called Earth

Come children sing the money song so

Weapons may dance on the graves of

Innocents sent by blind manufacturers

Generals dictators war lords gleefully

Anticipating profit and glorification from

The scorched devastated board game called

      Earth

Come children win this masochistic

Bloody board game called Earth

Come sing a last lonely plaintive song

Whose words have been forgotten

Whose melody is tremulous

Sing out before its memory dies

Come, sing the glorious song of

      Peace

Haunting and Haunted

by Marsha Warren Mittman

she hails from the Ukraine this slim slight

ephemeral woman with a haunting

haunted face and dark melancholy eyes

affected by the Chernobyl disaster as

a child she has numerous health issues

has become a rabid environmentalist

to mark Chernobyl's thirtieth year

she flew home from the States

where she's working on a PhD

still angry confused sad...and ill...

not trusting her raw emotions

over gruesome memories rekindled

and i recall my son's teenaged friend
on a group school trip years ago from
the United States to the Ukraine caught
in the midst of the catastrophic meltdown
back home checked every three months
but sadly long since gone by now

i give the haunted woman a photo
of two innocent toddlers, son and friend,
safely playing in my backyard and ask
that she place it in one of the many
memorials springing up in the Ukraine
wishing peace to those departed
wishing health to those affected
wishing wisdom for the future

#

by Marsha Warren Mittman

Red

      represents love, often
      depicted as a heart, but

Red

      also signifies blood,
      war, hatred, murder

Red

      newly symbolizing the loss
      of thousands of Native women
      kidnapped, missing, killed

Red

      the color of protest—their
      empty ghostly red dresses
      hung by rope from bare,
      stark, stripped dead trees

Red

      the color of friends' and
      relatives' eyes, crying from
      broken hearts, anxiously
      awaiting those they love

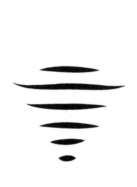

JACEK WILKOS is an engineer from Poland. He is addicted to buying books, he loves black coffee, dark ambient music and riding his bike. His work was published in numerous anthologies by Black Hare Press, Alien Buddha Press, Eerie River Publishing, Insignia Stories, Fantasia Divinity, Reanimated Writers Press, KJK publishing.

Facebook: @Jacek.W.Wilkos

Blossom

by Jacek Wilkos

The birds sing for joy,

warming up in the morning sun.

The colors of nature blossom

under a cloudless blue sky.

The ground trembles, the bird takes flight,

as raw war reality shatters the calm.

Countless military trucks roar of helplessness,

transporting bodies for cremation.

Spring has come.

EVIE GROCH supervises in Graduate Schools of Education. Her opinion pieces, humor, poems, short stories, & recipes have been published in the *New York Times, The SF Chronicle, The Contra Costa Times, The Journal, Games Magazine*, various anthologies and online. Her work has won her recognition and awards.

Summary of Senses

by Evie Groch

I'm the scent of the white Asiatic lilies
at the burial site, the salt in the tears
of the widow, the sweat on the brow
of the gravedigger, the ache in the heart
of the family.

I'm the strain in the arm of the pallbearer,
the worry etched in the forehead lines
of the siblings, and the smell of exhaust
as cars leave the cemetery.

I am the soft landing of the golden disk
whose yellow, orange and red rays spread
to blanket the hallowed grounds
with warmth, peace, and grace.

I am the sound of the rusty hinge
on the gate swinging shut,
locking in the memory of the last farewell.

I am the summary of senses in sorrow
present when words can't suffice,
hidden in moments of grief
evidenced by inaudible sobs and silent embraces.

F is for Fiction

by Evie Groch

In the fifth season,
the fall of light
produces false colors.
A fatal grace
fools me twice,
leaves me forever plucked.

I'm fortune's pawn at the
opposite end of happy,
falling to ash far from
the tree of life.

I slide down the shaft
like silver on glass,
follow the faces of strangers
to where I become
a feast for crows,
watching my funeral in beige.

Spare Me

by Evie Groch

Don't push me off the canvas,

don't paint me out of the picture.

Leave a corner for me: a bit of colour,

a shadow, a glimmer of hope and life,

and I'll be forever grateful,

for even the negative space.

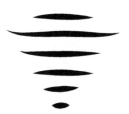

MAGGIE D. BRACE, a life-long denizen of Maryland, teacher, gardener, basketball player and author attended St. Mary's College, where she met her soulmate, and Loyola University, Maryland. She has written *'Tis Himself: The Tale of Finn MacCool* and *Grammy's Glasses*, and has multiple short works and poems in various anthologies. She remains a humble scrivener and avid reader.

Devouring Love

by Maggie D. Brace

In my slow descent into madness, I see you slip from my grasp.

Bit by bit, you've slowly turned your heart away from me, imperceptible at first,

then in gut churning obvious derision.

The two of us were one in body, soul, and mind.

You were my life, my everything, my reason for existing in this dark world.

Then, the unimaginable slowly manifested itself.

You sought to extricate yourself from me.

Finding fault with my mere existence, you slowly disengaged yourself.

Leaving me alone with my helpless devotion.

You held my crestfallen heart in your icy grasp.

Then, heedlessly crushed it into oblivion with your saturnine smile.

My life essence grinds to an uneasy halt.

I pray I can exist without you in my life,

unharmed by my devouring love.

ALISON BAINBRIDGE is a poet, author and PhD Candidate living in Newcastle, UK. Her poetry has been published in *Glitchwords, Wormwood Press Magazine, The Minison Project, Brave Voices Magazine* and *Off Menu Press,* while her short stories have appeared in *Daughters of Darkness (2019)* ed. Blair Daniels, *Mirror Dance Fantasy,* and *Revenant Journal.* Her poem "Sealskin Reclaimed" was nominated for a Rhysling Award in short poetry in 2020.

Twitter: @ally_bainbridge

The Seal-Wife's Daughter

by Alison Bainbridge

My father burned my mother's coat.
He said she looked too long at the sea—
too lovingly at the waves. They brought her gifts
of shells and glass worn down to jewels.
She kept them on the nightstand next to her
wedding ring and a bag filled with my baby teeth,
and she would count them every night before bed.

After the flames died, I took the ashes
and scattered them amongst dunes and rockpools.
I fed the charred remains of my mother's freedom
to the crabs. I wrapped my own coat, still fluffy white,
around her shoulders.

I keep the gifts the sea sends: glass jewels threaded
on strands of seaweed; bones and teeth and the remains
of monsters.

Wraith

by Alison Bainbridge

You moved in

a slow creeping; night

gathering over the sky.

Your shadows lengthened

until I lit a torch to scare you away.

I still find them

coiled in strange corners,

nesting at the bottom of my jewellery box.

I look for them when I miss you,

switch off the lights and let them

crawl back in

until I remember—

I don't miss you at all.

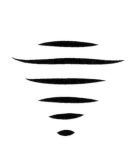

CHRIS BILES is a queer writer/artist currently living and working in Washington D.C. She enjoys playing with the light and the dark, and losing herself in music, anything outside, and some words here and there. Published by *Bourgeon Online*, Exeter Publishing, *Evening Street Review*, Haunted Waters Press, Yellow Arrow Publishing, *Signatures Magazine*, *FleasOnTheDog*, and others.

Website: www.chrisbiles03.com

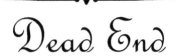

Dead End

by Chris Biles

Life's routine is like a straightaway on a country road.

On and on, beyond our sight, it continues,

and sometimes looking down that road makes you wonder

if it will ever end.

Most of the time, you just keep driving.

I just keep driving.

We

just keep driving.

But at some point, one of us will get brave

decide to open the door and jump

whether that means suicide or liberation

—both.

It will be at a crossroads

where the devil,

with a smile on his face,

waves his red flag to those he deems worthy.

One of us will open the car door—

abandon,

fly free—

prove him correct in his assumption.

And one of us

will drive on,

always looking back

in the rearview

until the road ends

—dead.

Then is when the realization will come

that we missed a sign way back in the beginning;

back when we first turned down this road.

On Being Watched By Birds

by Chris Biles

In my mind, my memory, your dark bird's eyes watch with the fear of prey in the presence of a predator. Intensions misconstrued. I only wanted to hold, help, love—stop you. But when I said "don't," there it was: fear. Eyes black like pools of ink not yet dry. In the fewer and fewer moments spent in my arms, you whispered, "every place I go, there I am," but I failed to comprehend the extent to which you needed to outrun yourself.

Every place you went, there you were—until—you woke in the darkness of early morning, left your warmth to linger then fade in our bed, stepped out into the dewy grass, with resolution bound your own hands, gagged your mouth, pushed your head beneath water, and simply sank.

Now, roaming the streets, deaths of despair ever-echo on the wind, and yours joins them, quietly: the seed of a dandelion at night rising with the breeze, unseen, yet of the same momentary glittering brilliance as a spider's web when it catches the moon. Glinting, glistening, drawn in ink not yet dry.

You are in the dark eyes of birds when they watch in fear. I try to tell them, try to explain: I only wanted to hold, help, stop—love you. But in love, we pick only the truths that seem sweetest. Often leaving the pocked and bruised bodies of the ugly fruits hanging, or fallen to the ground, unexplored. Devastatingly ignored.

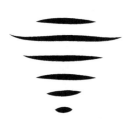

DJ ELTON writes fiction and lives in Sydney's Blue Mountains. Her work has been published with Clarendon House Books, Black Hare Press, Ravens Quoth Publishing, Iron Faerie Publishing, Spillwords, The Writer's Club and more. She stays connected, enjoys the wilderness, and is involved meditation-related projects when not writing.

Facebook: @djeltonwrites

The Mercy of Anna Lisa

by D.J. Elton

I   Enflamed

His deep blue eyes, such passionate skies, she was mesmerised.

The touch—an elegant hand, so cool—desires thrilling,

Unlocking great need, wanting nothing more.

Anna Lisa got *fluttery*, not knowing these feelings at all.

Dreamily, direly drifting, she scolded herself:

Tis a clear case of weakness

Having such an obsession for beauty in her life.

Yet the gentleman was a fake.

Twice they met in a café, and teahouse.

He'd asked her, candid and serene,

Was she unattached? Was her time available?

Would she meet him again?

Her personal details were so easily obtained.

In her trust as she absorbed his face,

His style, his voice, the movement of his hands—

O how they spun a cool tango.

An invitation; a seaside holiday at his grandaunt's.

She felt safe and secure, all thanks to him.

II Deception

Yet the gentleman callously tricked her.

He tripped her right up, getting into her soft inner place.

Made her think she was something wonderful. Adored by him.

Not frail, pale flesh, his true delight.

"Come with me," he implored, covering all traces.

None knew where she met him to hike.

They talked and walked until the sun was setting low.

Dusk—the sublime crossing time when anything can happen.

The sun settles and goes out of sight. Hidden, dark like him.

Shadowed—a creature of the night. He turned.

III   Turning

She gasped and wriggled, falling deeper into his binding.

His clean, glowing, sharp, little teeth.

That beautiful smile which he used to beguile—she knew
another side.

Tightly he held her, crushing her arms.

Cooed her name softly…sweetly, "Anna Lisa."

Seductively whispering as he sank a fierce bite

Into her luscious neck, so ripe,

Supped and drank his fill until she was faint.

"No more," she whispered. "Please, please."

He misunderstood; sank those bloody fangs again,

Deeply into her innocent breast.

Like a silent actress, she swooned—fell with him,

Crashing to the earth's floor. He swore,

Lay atop her—nothing doing for her modesty.

Completely drained, she flew far.

Far, far away from her body—a lifeless sack, robbed of its vital
red.

Stolen by him—her life—her last breath.

No gentleman was he, only a creature of lust and greed,

Who slithered, bloated, into the night.

IV   Redemption

Her life now gone. She sought to stay aground but couldn't.

Needing a cause—a plan. He became her reason to stay,

That gentleman who she knew was fake.

She watched him long on the earthly plane,

He lived five hundred years more,

Seeing his needs and habits.

When pale and sleeping, needing a redemptive death,

She decided to give him a new life.

Yet how could she raise a stake?

Hold up a cross?

Shower water holy to burn him?

She had no body to command such activities.

Some feeling stirred inside her.

Seeing him poor and lost, sad and heartbroken, so alone,

Despised by everyone, including himself.

That fake—that blood-eyed ungentleman.

V Atonement

He came her way again after many years passed.
And many maidens' veins were bled and dried by him.
Such a kindest wraith, Anna Lisa, saw him just as lost.
He was hopeless, helpless—his own tortured victim.
The stake finally took him—not by her hand.
Coming to her in spirit. *So sorry*—said he was not himself;
Cried and cried like a baby onto the ghostly neck of Anna Lisa,
Into her flowing hair, like mist, begging.
"O, Anna Lisa. Please have mercy."

MICHELE MEKEL wears many hats: educator, bioethicist, poetess, chief can opener, witch, and woman. Her work has appeared in various publications, been featured on Garrison Keillor's *The Writer's Almanac*, been nominated for Best of the Net, and been translated into Cherokee. She is co-principal investigator of *Viral Imaginations: COVID-19* (viralimaginations.psu.edu).

Drake Hotel, Chicago, November 2005

by Michele Mekel

I.

Reels of the mind flicker smoky blue—

> Rewind.

>> Replay.

>>> Repeat.

She knew this movie—*oh, so well*—

> Every actor.

>> Each line.

>>> Entirety of the scene.

II.

She saw him grab her hand tightly—*too tightly*—across the low
table—

> As the laughing couple at the far end of the atrium posed
> for wedding photos.

>> As the disinterested bartender polished glasses
>> with his starched apron.

>>> As heavy sleet pelted down on another
>>> November night.

She heard herself tell him that he could leave—

> Leave her city.

>> Leave her life.

>>> Leave her heart.

She witnessed him lean in closely, saying he'd have her—

> Have her hand.

>> Have her mind.

>>> Have her all.

She observed the sudden shift to "bullet time," a film effect that
happens occasionally in real life, too—

> Giving no answer.

>> Taking no breath.

>>> Allowing him to slip a ring on her finger
>>> in time-slice action.

III.

With each successive screening, she searched, hoping to spot the smallest delight in that "yes"—

A slight smile arising in the eyes.

A tiny, indrawn breath of joy.

Any sign of pleasant surprise.

Rather, there was always only—

Reeling.

Resignation.

Regret.

A version first published in *SPIT. Take II*, 2017

Tainted

by Michele Mekel

Under lore of the Snow Moon,
I wandered Goblin Market
ensconced in such a baleful wood.

Ghosts and ghouls of every ilk
pitched their pretty poisons
with much seductive appeal.

Yet, the one I sought
was not to be found
at either stand or stall.

Neither bribe nor promise
could conjure the toxic tonic
I feverishly required.

They had never heard of you.

First published in *MacroMicroCosm*,
2021

Skin Deep

by Michele Mekel

What if your misdeeds

were recorded as tattoos,

from brow to big toe?

Would we read of weakly denied dalliances—

accusing me of the same

in jarring, 2 a.m. outbursts?

Might "Malefactor" be written

in black, gothic font

across your collar bone?

Could the drinking

be depicted as overturned goblets

spilling Asian-motif waves of red wine?

And how should the end be rendered?

Perhaps, inside scrollwork with your penmanship,

among basic, flash-style roses:

"Angel, thanks for those years. Keep the ring."

As for me, you ask,

What of my wrongs?

Yes, turnabout is fair play.

It's simple.

The ink above my heart

would declare boldly in blood-red caps:

"STUPID."

Elixirs

by Michele Mekel

Sleep and solitude.
Food and drink.
I've badly abused

these restoratives
to escape the one
you poisoned—

love.

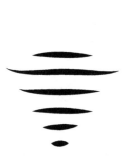

DANA TRICK Born a first-generation Mexican-Canadian-American autistic with ADHD, Dana Trick lives in Southern California where it is clearly foolish to wear black any day but she does it anyway. She wishes the reader a nice day.

You're Gone

by Dana Trick

I can't go out today.
I barely disturb these crinkled bed sheets
And the balls of tissues sprinkled on them.

Everyone put it in a child-friendly way;
  "They're in a better place"
Before they told me you died.

I don't want to know how you—
I want to know what you are
Going to do today?

If you are going to In-and-Out
After school, and if I could come with?

If your parents will finally
Let you come over during the weekend
To delve into our poisonous habits of procrastination
And inhale inhuman amounts of junk food,
All hidden under the guise of homework.

I want to see you
But…

TOM (WORDWULF) STERNER is a writer, vocalist and multi/media artist. A native of Colorado, he lives in Thornton, Colorado. His music, poetry, stories, artwork, and photography have been published in magazines and on the internet, including Howling Dog Press's *Omega*, *Skyline Literary Review*, New American Dream, The Storyteller, *Carpe Articulum Literary Review* and *Flashquake*.

Letters from the Monastery

by Tom (Wordwulf) Sterner

Will she remember me
in days to come
as the man of seven summers
Her words
and girlish excitement ignited
a frightful explosion in my heart
A handful of strawberries
and a beautiful woman;
I had no idea what they meant
For the rest of my life
they will wear her name

Sorrow is a temptress, a loaded gun lost
Got my finger on the trigger
Equanimity demands sanity, equilibrium
Being sane and sensible drives me crazy
The inmates are running the asylum,
arming our children, erasing their faces
I am a mad beast howling at road signs

When the night
pulls its mask o'er my face
I find it
ten-ton terrible to be alone
The monsters in my brain are afraid
They send minnows
out through my eyes
to chew holes
through the fabric of darkness
Life is a flesh-tone shroud we wear
to fool the mirror
Our face of death

There is a place where only we go,
this woman and me, and whenever I
am away from her, as I am now,
I go to that place
I am not so lonely
Though alone, it is good to know
she is there, for having her there,
never far away, there is still reason

The churchman has opened a door
A shaft of light divides his face
He chooses sides
to represent and support
his religion,
a proprietary bent toward
another man's woman
as if he hails from a house of lords
Fear owns the loose juice
of a man's bowels
The price he'd pay
to have done to them
what surely will
be done with him

I favor songs about hearts of stone,
the impenetrable forest,
man's id of trees,
pounding breasts, stomping feet,

howling epithets against the feral night
She twists nimbly through my senses,
frail and quick-footed, a nude dancer
into the churchman's hands,
the woman is a twelve-pound hammer

DARREN B. RANKINS began his writing career in sixth grade and became excited about poetry when the MTSU Honors Program Director suggested Darren take part in the 1994 MTSU Poetry Slam. He has since had publications in several magazines and newspapers. Darren also helps in his community by volunteering his extra time donating water and free photography for non-profit oganizations.

Website: purethoughts.info

The Memories of Yesterday

by Darren B. Rankins

The memories of yesterday… were the times we played, the days I came around just to see the smile on your face and how your smile told me why the sun shines.

The memories of yesterday… were the rainbows that I could never express, the way you made me feel. But to me, you were a living soul.

The memories of yesterday… are like thoughts today; loving, holding, and waiting to be with you—knowing all my dreams will come true.

The memories of yesterday… remind me of the last day I spent with you. I cried for the simple reason that I cared. Please remember me always. Your loving friend.

NATASHA ALVA is a first time poet and enjoys reading novels. She posts her poetry in her Instagram account and sometimes joins prompt contests from different poetry communities. As a silent type of person, poetry became her way of expressing her curiosity of feelings, words and observations of the world.

Instagram: @theburiedpages

Stuck

by Natasha Alva

I thought all these feelings would pass away.

I've cried all day long, and I still keep on saying that I will be okay; that all of this will end.

I keep pretending that nothing wrong happened.

I can't afford to bring in more drama.

I tend to keep quiet because the silence will lessen the problems.

Why do these mistakes keep coming back at me?

Have I already done enough?

I keep trying to make it alright but still end up getting it wrong.

How long do I have to keep on suffering; fooling myself all over again?

"It's okay," I say to myself.

"Just keep on smiling, even if it hurts."

"Just keep on trying, even if you're not yet ready."

Fight, fight.

I keep on hearing a certain voice in my sleep.

Fight, fight.

Even if the pain is hurting, I need to survive.

Fight, fight.

When can I win this battle for once?

Fight, fight.

When can I truly be happy again?

When can this façade finally fade into spring?

I don't know how long I can hide these feelings.

I cannot keep my act any longer but, I'll hold on until I can.

For now, I just have to keep on fighting.

I guess experiences needed to happen.

One day all those answers will come.

Until then, my heart, mind, and soul must keep fighting.

RENATA PAVREY is a nutritionist and Pilates teacher, marathon runner and Odissi dancer. Her stories, essays, poetry and artwork have featured in anthologies by Ghost Orchid Press, Black Ink Fiction, Sweetycat Press and Ravens Quoth Press, among others. She has a solo poetry collection titled, *Eunoia*.

Twitter: @writerlylegacy

The Outcast

by Renata Pavrey

Standing in the shadows

A candle that provides warmth

but doesn't light up the dark

Flaming without a sound

Melting

It disappears

A sunrise that doesn't

bring forth a new day

A fiery orb; it watches

from a distance

Unseen, unheard

but very much there

Scalding and scorching

It disappears

Pain and misery

camouflaged in hope

An outcast pleading

for a shred of mercy

A road travelled on

time and again

Different places

but the people are the same

Can't be buried or burned

if you weren't around to be gone

As soon as you belong

It's time to disappear

I See Light

by Renata Pavrey

Drowning and submerging

Chains coiled around my feet

The horizon heavily fading

For a dreary end to meet

Water bearing loneliness and despair

As it chokes my nose and mouth

Struggling to breathe and think

Throttled with no better way out

But then my teary eyes see

A shimmering orb in the distance

A glimmer of hope beckons

Telling me it brings assistance

Air of love and faith awaits

To fight back what water holds

See the light of the sun

Let it embrace you in its folds

Sinking low as it pulls you up

A sunset doesn't end at dusk

It paves way for a new sunrise

The universe always up for its task

Look forward to another day

Just as the sun invariably does

Don't say "goodbye" forever

Tomorrow awaits us.

JOSEPH A. FARINA is a retired lawyer and award-winning poet, in Sarnia, Ontario, Canada. His poems have appeared in *Philadelphia Poets*, *Tower Poetry*, *The Windsor Review*, and *Tamaracks: Canadian Poetry for the 21st Century*. He has two books of poetry published, *The Cancer Chronicles* and *The Ghosts of Water Street*.

Departures in the Rain

by Joseph A. Farina

almost broke down

almost spoke your name

she was on the crosstown bus

wearing her hair like yours

stopped at Erie and Ouellette

as I walked by one misted night

in Windsor under a winter rain

she was sitting by the window

half obscured by condensation

her breath visible like filaments of cloud

the dull bus light shadowing her eyes

I turned to search her face

but she disappeared into the cold mist

like you did so long ago

and though I wanted to forget you

I still whispered to your shadows

(the ones I stole before you left)

they did not speak to me

the streets are emptying

hand in hand, lovers are heading

for their doorways and disappear

except for me and others

who share a common thread

we shuffle under night rain

and hide our faces in shadows

cast by hydro moons

their cold light conducting our direction

to our desperate rooms

we dissolve there

into the waiting nothingness

of our individual oblivion

where touch does not intrude

senses never bleed

and eyes become blind

to incursive visions

in windows streaked with rain

MCKENZIE RICHARDSON lives in Milwaukee, WI. Her poetry can be found in Ravens Quoth Press' *Dream*. Her fiction has been published by Eerie River Publishing, Black Ink Fiction, and Iron Faerie Publishing.

She currently works in a library, doing her best not to be buried beneath an ever-growing TBR list.

Facebook: @mckenzielrichardson

The City We Built

by McKenzie Richardson

We built up our skyscrapers

    brick by brick

Carrying loads on our backs

    stone by stone

We twisted the metal with our bare hands

    then stared in shock

    at the sight of our own blood

These walls gave us the illusion of safety

    when really, they just kept us chained to ourselves.

Fragile windows shatter in our too-tight grip

    choke the life out of this structure

As explosions of glass

    dance around our faces

    like a firework show over the lake

We tried all we could to build up a city

    but it seems we only forged our own prison

A township of cages to barricade ourselves within

    but they couldn't keep us safe from each other.

It's difficult to relearn how to love

    and maybe it's too much to change our ways

Our routine too ingrained in our veins

    the muscle memory that rules our hearts

    moving us on its own accord

Always falling back into our own learned helplessness

    reaching, reaching, never quite touching

I'm sorry I couldn't love that way anymore

    I had to let our city crumble.

The Tongue

by McKenzie Richardson

This forked tongue speaks multitudes.

Which path will this snake travel down?

How to choose at a fork in the road

you can't always smell your way down the right course.

Wrap your tongue 'round your mind

like a woodpecker.

Your words are what keep you safe.

Cushion the blow when your walls crash down

and you're left without a single feather.

Use that tongue to speak out now.

Use that tongue to demand change.

Lap up the blood that seeps from their wounds

and never again accept their blame.

My Heart Houses an Empty Shelf

by McKenzie Richardson

My heart houses an empty shelf for memories stored—
> stories never passed on,
> the history of a people that died in secrecy.

We lived between silent walls
> where the shadows watched but did not retain.

My heart houses an empty shelf of all the stories you did not tell—
> memories never given voice,
> starved for air between silent walls.

Where there are ears to listen—
> tell your story,
> share your history.

I had so much room to hold you
> but you never claimed that space within me.

Now time has stolen what was left
> and that shelf remains forever empty.

Broken Things

by McKenzie Richardson

This family collects broken things.

Spare parts and broken hearts,
pool ladders without a home,
tattered books and cast-off looks,
and people worn to the bone.

We've got broken clocks, mismatched socks,
furniture from the side of the road,
fabric scraps and forgotten laughs,
and those who've abandoned the load.

Now we've cluttered up every corner
with things once left behind.
When I squeeze through the door, I see
a house no longer mine.

This family collects broken things,
but it seems they're getting choosey.
When I broke into pieces,
they did not make room for me.

GRETA SHARKEY is a writer, poet, editor, educator, researcher, artist, and Professor Emerita at Nassau Community College. I am currently serving on the editorial staff of *45 Magazine*, an online women's journal. My writing has appeared in several journals and in the anthology, *Songs of Seasoned Women* edited by Patti Tana.

Website: angelwords7.wixsite.com/greta-sharkey-

Visits to My Mother

by Greta Sharkey

After I was grown,

I used to visit my mother for tea

in blue flowered cups

with thin and fragile handles.

The afternoons squeezed themselves in

between swiftly flying mornings

and dark mysterious nights.

She'd set the table

on a white embroidered cloth

that my hands had sewn.

Worn a bit and stained with tea,

it would recline beneath our conversations

of politics and lilacs

and sleep its uneasy sleep,

waiting for the end of chatter.

But then when she fell,

they took her away

and the house stayed empty,

waiting for tea—in silence.

I would pass and look back,

wishing there were someone

I could stop for, and then

traveled to the place where

she waited and slept

beneath an unfamiliar roof.

Holding her soft hand,

brushing her hair from her brow,

I watched and waited.

The Wounds

by Greta Sharkey

Scared, pale,
remembering and losing memory,
life has not left us the blank slate
they once told us we had been—but never were.
Our pages were not only written on
in ways we never expected,
but marked and torn,
yellowed and stained in blood—not always our own.
We brought some of them with us
through the womb.
Others were won
on the battlefields and flood banks.
Some words we wrote in sweat and tears.
Others were written for us in invisible ink
for us to find when we held them up
to the light.
But they all are ours now,
the wounds we have come to know
as our stories.
The wounds we could no longer
live without.

The Empty Spaces

by Greta Sharkey

The empty spaces in a room,

in the heart, in the soul,

will shrink with time,

but never go away.

Others will enter the spaces

we reserved for those

who are no longer here,

but those spaces will always belong

to our memories—then, now and in the making.

ANNE CAPRICE CLAROS is a Filipino-Canadian poet who creates from her experiences lines of poetry which she hopes will move and inspire self-reflection and even healing in her readers. Her work has been published numerously by *juice Journal,* and appears as well in editions of *Existential Ponders, The Quilliad, Herion Love Songs* and *The Wild Word.* This year, Anne was one of twelve poets who won the *2022 Writes of Spring Contest* hosted by *The Winnipeg International Writers Festival* and *The Winnipeg Free Press.* Her winning poem was featured in the April 24th, Sunday Edition, of *The Winnipeg Free Press.*

Empty Lullaby

by Anne Caprice Claros

I stare into the black and

blue bruised sky

framed by the dead-white

soulless skeleton

of my bedroom window.

Starless—even the moon hid

from tonight's desertion.

The night has abandoned me too

I reach into the barren shadow

that shamelessly spilled all over

my city. How many eyes are witness

tothis neglect? I reach further

and further into thinning air. I wait

for a warm touch to reach back,

wrap around me and hum me to sleep.

Unsent Letter

by Anne Caprice Claros

I keep a picture of you—
of us, standing side by side
on our high school field bleachers.
I look at it too
often. I feel obligated
to confess.
But if the church won't forgive
me, neither should

you; a dreamy seventeen-year-old
in an unbuttoned plaid shirt
and a black crewneck tee.
Your hair caramel
against the brass sunset
that hatches over faded roofs.
Your eyes hold forests captive.
The Elms that guard River Heights'
aged streets must be envious
of their unbounded life.
Your lips bleed sugar

and I can't rid myself of the sweet
aftertaste of your kisses.
A glass of water.
A bottle of mouthwash.
A shot of alcohol.
Even the spit of strangers can't
purge me of you.

I sit alone.
My fingers fade the borders of
our photograph. Happy
twenty-second birthday.
Has it really been five years?
How many more

men must I welcome
into my bed to numb myself
from the sting of the mint
in your aftershave?

Irreparable

by Anne Caprice Claros

I think I am broken.

A shattered beer bottle

after one too many. A mistake

swept up, dumped and forgotten.

      I am beautiful.

I catch the light—

make fragmented rainbows.

Don't

touch me.

I will cut you.

I will leave a scar.

Go and tell your friends

about it years later,

over beers. I will

never be again.
I try to tell my best friend
        she is beautiful,
but I see my lips crumble away.
I see myself—scattered pieces—
    recognisable and
unrecognisable.
Can you be two things at once?
I am

a sandcastle reclaimed by the sea
before your mom could see
and before your dad could
pat you on the back.
I am a wave diminished by the shore.
Pieces of me burst—
bubbles into oblivion.

Are you okay?
                I lie.
I sweat alcohol. I reek.
I am ugly.
I spill. I am spilling.
I keep together like water.
Mop me up.
Clean me up. Clean

me. I feel dirty.

I have bumpy lines on my skin;

dried up glue that leaked from my cracks.

They tried to fix me.

Now, I am uglier.

Don't you get it?

Broken means free,

like your unfinished beer

that splashed all over

when the bottle slipped,

kissed the ground, and smashed.

Kisses smash you up.

Kiss me and make a mess.

Let me pool on the floor.

I will evaporate by morning.

An Elegy

by Anne Caprice Claros

The page bled as I scratched and punctured its surface.

My pen clearly marked its wake

as it slowly marched from left to right.

Each stroke, a glacial movement destined to leave a scar.

As its wounds clotted and dried,

bound within them were thoughts made immortal

in the hopes that one day, they too will be great.

How foolish.

These thoughts turned to words

were not my thoughts nor my words,

but traces of a poison

forced down my throat;

echoes of what *must* be said.

Echoes of what the world *wants* to hear.

They have infested my mind with lies

and anchored my voice with judgement.

They have killed my tongue.

My soul lay among the ashes—

remnants of the fire over which my heart hung.

An angry fire in the epicenter of a crowd

hungry to feast. And feast they did.

So turn the page,

for herein lies no unthinkable secret,

no unworldly knowledge,

but a procession of words

that solemnly skirt a silken black hearse

in which a poet rests—a silenced poet

whose voice the world chooses to ignore.

THE RAVENS QUOTH PRESS is a boutique publisher based in Australia, dedicated to showcasing the best of international poetry craft in beautifully presented publications.

Follow us: linktr.ee/TheRavensQuothPress

Printed in Great Britain
by Amazon

82877279R00140